THE JUBILEE BIBLE STUDY GUIDE

The Jubilee Bible Study Guide

Enoch Lavender

Olive Tree Ministries

Contents

How to Use This Book   vii

1	The Jubilee Gospel	1
2	The Jubilee Restoration	9
3	The Jubilee Trumpet	15
4	The Jubilee Return	18
5	The Jubilee Resurrection	23

How to Use This Book

Welcome to the Jubilee Bible Study series.

Understanding the topic of the Jubilee has revolutionised my personal understanding of Jesus ministry, and I pray you will also be blessed as you join me in this study.

This series consists of five 10-15 minute long videos introducing each chapter. For best results:

- Watch one video session at a time
- Work your way through the questions and notes for that chapter.

These study notes are suitable for use in a Bible study group or for your own personal devotion.

You can access the videos via the QR code on the right or at www.olivetreeministries.tv/jubilee.

Come and join me as we begin our study in Chapter 1.

Yours in Messiah,
Enoch Lavender
Olive Tree Ministries

1

The Jubilee Gospel

Before You Start

Watch the video for this chapter first and then work your way through these questions as we dig deeper into the topic.

Video link:
www.olivetreeministries.tv/jubilee or scan the QR code on the right.

Jesus and the Jubilee

In today's video we were introduced to the topic of the Jubilee and saw how it is about restoring people to freedom and to their God-given inheritance.

Let's study this topic further in light of Jesus' ministry in the New Testament.

> Jesus went about all Galilee, teaching in their synagogues, and **preaching the gospel of the kingdom**, and **healing** all manner of sickness and all manner of disease (*Matthew 4:23*)

Now He was teaching in one of the synagogues on the Sabbath. [11]And behold, there was a woman who had a spirit of infirmity eighteen years, and was bent over and could in no way raise herself up. [12]But when Jesus saw her, He called her to Him and said to her, "Woman, you are loosed from your infirmity." [13]And He laid His hands on her, and immediately she was made straight, and glorified God. (*Luke 4:10-13*)

Study Questions

#1: In light of these verses, in what ways did Jesus fulfill the Jubilee?

#2: In what other ways do you think Jesus fulfilled the Jubilee?

Disappointed in Jesus

¹³ Now behold, two of them were traveling that same day to a village called Emmaus.. ¹⁵ So it was, while they conversed and reasoned, that Jesus Himself drew near and went with them. ¹⁶ But their eyes were restrained, so that they did not know Him.

¹⁷ And He said to them, "What kind of conversation *is* this that you have with one another as you **walk and are sad**?"

¹⁸ Then the one whose name was Cleopas answered... "The things concerning Jesus of Nazareth... **we were hoping that it was He who was going to redeem Israel.**"
(*Luke 24:13-21*)

The disciples were crushed and sad, not only because Jesus had died, but also because they had expected that He would redeem Israel. They clearly believed He had failed to bring the Jubilee foretold by the prophets.

#3: In what ways did Jesus NOT fulfill the Jubilee?

Future Fulfilment

The prophecies about Jesus' first coming were very literally fulfilled. For example, He was literally born in Bethlehem and He literally experienced an agonizing death as foretold in great detail by the prophets.

> #4: If Jesus literally fulfilled so much Old Testament prophecy during His first coming, is it reasonable to expect that He will fulfil the remaining prophecies of the Jubilee literally? Or do they apply in more of a spiritual sense only? Explain your answer.

WHEN IS THE JUBILEE?

After Jesus' resurrection, He spent 40 days with the disciples teaching about the Kingdom.

At the end of this teaching, the disciples had one burning question to ask:

> "Lord, will You at this time restore the kingdom to Israel (i.e. the Jubilee)?" Acts 1:6.

Some theologians teach that this question showed how the disciples still did not understand Jesus' teachings. But Jesus did not dismiss their question as being invalid and off topic. Jesus simply replied that it was not for them to know 'the time and the season' which the Father has in His own hand (Act 1:7).

Peter must still have had this question in mind as he got up to preach a few days later on the Day of Pentecost. Inspired by the Holy Spirit, Peter had this to say about the Jubilee prophecies and the timing of this coming restoration:

> [19] "Therefore, repent and turn to God, so that your sins may be erased; [20] so that times of refreshing may come from the Lord's presence; and he may send the Messiah appointed in advance for you, that is, Yeshua. [21] He has to remain in heaven until the **time comes for restoring everything,** as God said long ago, when he spoke through the holy prophets. (Acts 3:19-21)

The 'restoration of everything' refers to the Jubilee prophecies of the Old Testament Prophets and Peter links this restoration directly to the time of the Messiah's return.

Question 5: According to Peter, what are the conditions for this End Time Jubilee to take place?

> Question 6: Are we getting closer to this final restoration now? List reasons why or why not.

LOOK UP

Large portions of the Church have had a dark, pessimistic view of the End Times.

> Question 7: List some of the dark and evil things foretold to happen in the End Times:

In the middle of Jesus' End Time prophecies, He gives us the following important statement:

> Now when these things begin to happen, look up and lift up your heads, because your redemption (or Jubilee) draws near. (Luke 21:28)

In another passage, Jesus similarly talks about the 'joy' coming after the trials of the End Times:

²¹ A woman, when she is in labor, has sorrow because her hour has come; but as soon as she has given birth to the child, she no longer remembers the anguish, for joy that a human being has been born into the world.
(John 16:21)

Question 8: In light of the Jubilee and End Time Prophecy in general, what joyful events are we to look forward to with Jesus' return? How do these events outweigh the final dark days of this current world system?

MAKING IT PERSONAL

Like Israel, many of us have gone through personal loss and suffering. We have endured sickness, and grief.

Consider any personal areas where you or your family / community need restoration, and join me in prayer:

Father God, I come to you in the Name of Jesus.

I present before you the broken situation in my life of ......
Jesus, thank you that you are not only Israel's Redeemer, but also my Redeemer.

I thank you that in all things you work for my good as I love you (Rom. 8:28), and I believe you are going to take the evil out of this situation. For those who may have hurt me and sinned against me, I choose to forgive them right now (be specific as you pray)

Satan, hands off my ..... in Jesus mighty name!

Thank you Jesus that you are a God of restoration. Thank you for coming to not only save me, but also to redeem me and restore all that the enemy has taken away from me.

I receive it now, in Jesus mighty Name,
Amen!

2

The Jubilee Restoration

Before You Start

Watch the video for this chapter first and then work your way through these questions as we dig deeper into the topic.

Video link: www.olivetreeministries.tv/jubilee or scan the QR code on the right.

The Restoration of Israel and the Church

In today's study, we have looked at the Dual Restoration of Israel and the Church over the last 150 years.

Key events of this restoration have happened in a Jubilee like time-frame – i.e.

- 1917: Britain issues the Balfour declaration paving the way for the creation of the State of Israel in 1948
- 1967: Jerusalem is conquered by Israel in the miraculous 6 Day War.
- 2017: President Trump and the US recognise Jerusalem as the capital of Israel and move their embassy, culminating a series of peace agreements between Israel and her Arab neighbours.

> Question 1: The one big missing piece in this restoration is Israel's Temple. Do you think this will be restored at all? If so, will it be before or after the Messiah comes? Why?

THE DUAL RESTORATION

In today's teaching, we have seen how Israel and the Church have been going through a parallel restoration.

> Question 2: What do you think would be the next restoration for the Church?

> Question 3: What can we do to help bring about this restoration?

OPPOSING THE RESTORATION

The Restoration of the Church back to the teaching and power found in the New Testament has faced a lot of opposition.

Sadly, this opposition has often come from established churches evicting those who embrace fresh revelation from the Bible. For example, the Baptists were forced out for their teaching on baptism. Many years later, they in turn expelled those who embraced speaking in tongues. And in this way the pattern has continued with each fresh wave of revelation.

> Question 4: How can we learn from history and avoid opposing future moves of God's restoration?

> Question 5: Has God finished restoring the Church now – or should we expect further restoration to happen? What would this restoration look like?

GOD'S MERCY

The restoration of Israel so far has been without a major repentance on her behalf or a turning towards God.

Question 6: Why do you think God has been restoring Israel in recent years without them first turning to Him in repentance?

Question 7: How far do you think God will restore Israel at this stage? What will only be restored to her once she fully turns back to God?

Question 8: Paul says that Israel's turning away from God has brought salvation to the world, but that her restoration will bring 'life from the dead' (Rom 11:11-15). What do you think this 'life from the dead' means for us and the world?

MAKING IT PERSONAL

The restoration of Israel and the Church is central to God's plans and purposes for the End Times and for His Return. Will you join with me as we pray:

Dear God,

Thank you that in your mercy you have been restoring Israel and the Church. We pray for Israel that you will continue to regather her to her land and to fulfill your good promises to this nation. We pray for the eyes of the Jewish people to be opened and their hearts prepared to welcome you back as their Messiah.

Thank you Lord for the restoration of the Church that has been taking place. Help us not to stand in the way of future restorations but give us humble hearts to discern what you are doing in your Church today.

Lord, let us be part of the movement of restoration that you are doing today. Give us fresh understanding and revelation of your Word and your Ways. We pray this in Jesus Name, Amen

FURTHER STUDY

For further study, see the following resources:

6 Day War

Watch Teaching Video at www.olivetreeministries.tv/6daywar (or scan the below qr code to visit the link)

The Third Temple

See our book *'Rebuilding The Temple: Preparing the Way for the Lord's Return'* by Enoch Lavender.

Available via Amazon or www.olivetreeministries.tv

3

The Jubilee Trumpet

Before You Start

Watch the video for this chapter first and then work your way through these questions as we dig deeper into the topic.

Video link: www.olivetreeministries.tv/jubilee or scan the QR code on the right.

The Jubilee Trumpet and End Times

In today's teaching we have discovered:

- The Jubilee is announced with the sounding of the Trumpet
- Exodus chapter 19 pre-figures Jesus' Return – at the sound of the Trumpet
- The exact date of His Return is unknown, but we should live ready.

> Question 1: If the Jubilee is linked to Jesus' Return, what should we expect His Return to look like?

> Question 2: Why shouldn't we set dates for Jesus' possible Return?

> Question 3: Exodus 19:10-15 involved three days of preparation and cleansing before the visible descent of God's glory on Mt Sinai. In what ways can we prepare ourselves for the Messiah's Return?

MAKING IT PERSONAL

Jewish brides at the time of Jesus were trained to wait for their bridegrooms to come unexpectedly, and often even in the middle of the night. They therefore had to live ready, with their bridal dresses and lamps ready for the day (or night) when the groom would arrive.

The trumpet blast would announce the coming of the groom, much like the trumpet will one day announce the coming of Jesus.

Are you ready for His Return?

Let's pray together.

Lord Jesus,
We thank you that you have promised to come again.
We pray that you will prepare us for your return, and that you will help us to always live ready for that great day.

Lord, where our lives have become polluted by this world, please forgive us. We repent of our sin including ... and receive your forgiveness now. Through the power of your Spirit we choose to turn back to you and to live ready for Your Coming.

In Jesus Name, Amen

4

The Jubilee Return

Before You Start

Watch the video for this chapter first and then work your way through these questions as we dig deeper into the topic.

Video link: www.olivetreeministries.tv/jubilee or scan the QR code on the right.

The Final Ingathering

In today's Bible study, we have examined one of the most common themes of Old Testament prophecy, which is the Final Ingathering of the Jewish people to their ancient homeland.

We have seen how this links in with the ultimate Jubilee and the restoration of the land to its original owners. We have also seen how this restoration is going to be linked to the final restoration of Israel to her God.

We ended the session by asking the question: "Where is this major prophetic theme found in the New Testament writings?"

HIDDEN IN PLAIN SIGHT

Bible Prophecy in the New Testament heavily relies on and builds on the foundation given throughout the rest of the Scriptures.

Jeremiah 16:14-16 proclaims that there is a greater Exodus to come than the original Exodus. In other words, it is going to be exceedingly more spectacular and more miraculous than Israel's departure from Egypt some 3500 years ago.

Jesus' disciples would have been extremely familiar with this and similar prophecies of the Hebrew Scriptures.

Keeping this in mind, let's consider for a moment how they would have heard Jesus' words about the End of Days:

> 29"Immediately after the tribulation of those days .... the sign of the Son of Man will appear in heaven, and then **all the tribes of the earth** (Hebrew meaning – 'all the tribes of the land of Israel') will mourn, and they will see the Son of Man coming on the clouds of heaven with power and great glory. 31And He will send His angels with a great sound of a trumpet, and they will **gather together His elect** from the four winds, from one end of heaven to the other.
> (Matt 24:29-31)

Jesus' Jewish listeners would most likely have understood His reference to 'all the tribes of the earth' as referring to Israel. This is because in Hebrew the word translated 'earth' is 'aaretz', and this word almost always refers specifically to the geographic Land of Israel.

> Question 1: Putting aside for a moment your own view of the Rapture, what do you think the disciples would have understood these verses to mean?

It is possible that the Rapture involves not only the Church meeting Jesus in the air, but the Jewish people also being regathered to Israel.

> Question 2: Discuss what the sequence of End Time events may look like from this perspective.

MAKING IT PERSONAL

We have today explored the Rapture and the Final Ingathering of Israel in a way that will be new to many of us. May I encourage you to search out the Scriptures for yourself on this topic while praying for further revelation.

Jesus,
We thank you that you will one day regather and restore your people Israel, and we thank you for your promise to one day come for your Church.
We pray that you will prepare Israel for your Return as King, and that you will give us understanding of your coming Kingdom.

Lord, we don't want to fight our fellow believers over different understandings of the Rapture and End Times. However, we pray that you will reveal to us your truth as we study your Word.

May your Kingdom come, and your will be down on earth as it is in Heaven.

In Jesus Name,
Amen

Further Study

For further study, see the following resource:

Regathering of Israel and the Final Trumpet

Teaching video at www.olivetreeministries.tv/regathering (or scan the below qr code to visit the link)

5

The Jubilee Resurrection

Before You Start

Watch the video for this chapter first and then work your way through these questions as we dig deeper into the topic.

Video link: www.olivetreeministries.tv/jubilee or scan the QR code on the right.

The Resurrection

In today's study, we have examined the topic of the Resurrection as part of the Jubilee and linked it to the sounding of the Jubilee trumpet.

As in the words of Paul the Apostle:

> "For the trumpet will sound, the dead will be raised imperishable, and we will be changed"
> (1 Cor 15:52)

In other words, the final Jubilee will include a dramatic restoration on many levels, including the restoration of our dead bodies, the restoration of inheritance and land, and the restoration of the Kingdom to Israel.

THE HOPE OF THE RESURRECTION

Around 170 years before Jesus, a terrible wave of persecution broke out in Israel. The book of Maccabees records the powerful stories of some of the heroic martyrs of this time. In their own words, these martyrs explained that their motivation was the Hope of the Resurrection.

Likewise, in Lyon in Ad 170, Jesus' followers went through crushing persecution. The Romans noted amongst themselves how it was their belief in the resurrection which enabled them to hold firm even when threatened with death.

> Question 1: In what way do you think the message of the physical resurrection motivated these heroes of the faith?

IF THERE IS NO RESURRECTION

In 1 Cor 15:12-55 Paul debates those who argue that there is no physical resurrection of the body. Notice these key statements of Paul concerning the resurrection:

> ...if the dead do not rise, then Christ is not risen.... ...If in this life only we have hope in Christ, we are of all men the most pitiable.
> (1 Cor 15:16, 19)

> Question 2: In your own words, explain Paul's statement above.

WASHING DEAD BODIES?

Ancient Jewish burial customs include washing the dead body, anointing it with expensive perfumes and wrapping it in cloth (see John 19:40, Acts 9:37 for NT examples). Then the body would be laid in a tomb, and the mourner will have to go through a ritual cleansing (a baptism) because of handling the dead body.

This is why Paul asks:

> 'If the dead are not raised at all, why are people baptized for them?'
> (1 Cor 15:29)

> Question 3: Why did the Jewish people go through this difficult, expensive and time-consuming process for the sake of a dead body?

> Question 4: To this day, Jewish people try to get buried in the land of Israel itself, and if possible on the Mount of Olives. Why do you think they do this?

MAKING IT PERSONAL

At the end of today's teaching video, I mentioned the Hope of the Resurrection. The hope of not only having our lives restored, but also having the lives of our loved ones restored and of meeting them again in the flesh.

Personally, this message gave me great comfort during a time of grief over the loss of a loved one. I pray that you too will find comfort in these words of hope in our Messiah.

Let me pray with you for a moment.

Lord Jesus,
I thank you for those who have joined me for this Bible Study on the Jubilee. I pray that the truths of your Word will stick deep into our hearts and will motivate us as it did the early believers.

I pray specifically for those who have been grieving over the loss of a loved one. I pray that you will comfort them and fill them with a very real sense of hope that they will one day see their loved ones again.

I thank you Jesus that you are the Resurrection and the Life and together we look forward to the great and final Jubilee yet to come.

In Jesus name,
Amen

FURTHER STUDY

For further study, see the following resources:

Hanukkah and Courage in Persecution

Teaching video at www.olivetreeministries.tv/hanukkah (or scan the below qr code to visit the link)

The Resurrection vs Heaven

Teaching video at www.olivetreeministries.tv/resurrection (or scan the below qr code to visit the link)

www.ingramcontent.com/pod-product-compliance
Lightning Source LLC
Chambersburg PA
CBHW072339300426
44109CB00042B/1958